The Road to a New Countryside

Wang Tai Zhao Jingyu Li Haitao

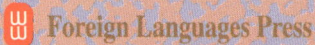
Foreign Languages Press

First Edition 2007

ISBN 978-7-119-05133-8
© Foreign Languages Press, Beijing, China, 2007
Published by Foreign Languages Press
24 Baiwanzhuang Road, Beijing 100037, China
Website: http: //www.flp.com.cn
Email Addresses: Info@flp.com.cn
Sales@flp.com.cn
Distributed by China International Book Trading Corporation
35 Chegongzhuang Xilu, Beijing 100044, China
P. O. Box 399, Beijing, China

Printed in the People's Republic of China

CONTENTS

A New Chapter on an Old Subject   *1*

How Far Are We from Agricultural Modernization?   *17*

A New Look for Ancient Villages   *49*

Blue Skies over City and Country   *63*

Farmers Hang Up Their Farm Tools   *79*

Who Cultivates Culture?   *95*

Seeking Dynamics from Farmers   *105*

The Road to a
New Countryside

1

A New Chapter on an Old Subject

January 28, 2006, was the Spring Festival Eve, the 30th day of the 12th month on the lunar calendar. It is the most important traditional Chinese festival when families get together to welcome in the New Year. On that day though, Hu Jintao, general secretary of the CPC Central Committee and president of China, visited the home of Kang Haifa, a villager in Hougoumen Village, Yanhewan Town, Ansai County, a mountainous region of Shaanxi Province. He personally fried New Year cakes (made of glutinous rice flour) for the family, and even stayed to try the cakes and drink some piping hot rice wine. On the same day, Premier Wen Jiabao went to Guozhuang Village on the outskirts of Heze City, Shandong Province, where he met with villagers to make dumplings and see in the New Year.

This is the third year that Chinese state leaders have spent this most important festival at farmers' homes to show their deep concern for farmers and rural areas.

In March 2006, at the 4th Session of the 10th National People's Congress (NPC), an agreement was reached on the "Outline for the 11th Five Year Plan (2006-2010) for the National Economic and Social Development of the People's Republic of China (PRC)." This document consists of 14 chapters, of which the chapter "Building a New Socialist Countryside" comes first in order to show its prominence. The chapter lays out the importance of building a new socialist countryside and what

◆ A pearl farm in Huaibei City, Anhui Province.

economic gap between urban and rural areas has started to grow.

Statistics show that, between 1990 and 2004, the per-capita income of farmers increased by an average of 4.6%, 1.6 times slower than in the 1980s. In the same period, the per-capita income of urban residents increased by an average of 7.6% per year, or 65% faster than that of farmers.

◆ A Uyghur villager and his new tractor.

Moreover, because state funds had been largely channeled into urban areas, problems with transportation, drinking water, fuel and electricity in rural areas were becoming more pronounced. These problems could not be resolved due to a lack of sufficient funds. Rural areas were also lagging far behind urban areas in social welfare, education and healthcare. By 2005, half of China's administrative villages did not have tap water, over 60% of rural households did not have hygienic toilets and 150 million farmers had trouble obtaining fuel. There are four times as many rural secondary students as urban secondary school students, but the rural students only enjoyed 38% of the educational fees paid by the state. Since 2003, although nearly half of all farmers receive a government subsidy for medical expenses, over half are still uninsured and must pay for it themselves.

The widening gap between urban and rural areas is affecting China's economic development. Some economists believe if farmers' incomes are too low it will be impossible to create a market for China's industrial goods. Insufficient internal demand would hinder industrial development.

There is no doubt that the problems of agriculture, rural areas and farmers (the "three rurals") will have to be dealt with urgently if China is to continue to develop.

In 2004, a series of positive steps were taken for

◆ A bird's-eye view of terraced fields.

the Chinese countryside. In January, the CPC Central Committee and the State Council published the report "Suggested Policies to Increase the Income of Farmers." This document is seen as of vital importance in increasing the income of farmers in the main grain-producing areas. In March, Premier Wen Jiabao declared in his "Work Report of the Government" at the 2nd Session of the 10th National People's Congress that agricultural production would be exempted from tax within five years. In 2004, 25 provinces, autonomous regions and municipalities cancelled agricultural taxes. This policy profited all of China's 730 million farmers: some by a few dozen yuan and some by hundreds of yuan. In September, at the 4th Plenary Session of the 16th CPC Central Committee, General Secretary Hu Jintao reiterated that China had reached a stage of development where industry sustains agriculture and cities support the countryside. In December, the Central Rural Work Conference said that if we are to solve the problems of the "three rurals", we must "give more, take less and remove obstacles."

From agriculture sustaining industry to industry sustaining agriculture, from the countryside serving cities to cities bringing along the countryside, the Chinese government is seeking a best solution to the problems facing rural development.

Statistics show that in 2004 the Chinese economy

maintained a growth rate of as high as 9.5%, while the per-capita net income of farmers grew by 6.8%, the highest rate over the last few years. Through a series of positive measures the Chinese government is gradually resolving the antagonism between urban and rural economic development and the problems related specifically to rural development.

At the end of 2005, the CPC Central Committee and the State Council published "Suggestions for Developing Modern Agriculture and for the Construction of a New Socialist Countryside." This document consists of eight parts which comprise 32 articles. It sets forth a detailed series of measures for building a new countryside, and calls on local governments to bring this plan to fruition and to quicken the pace of construction. In 2006, the state invested 339.7 billion yuan in supporting agriculture, 40 billion yuan more than in 2005. On top of that, in 2006, agricultural tax was completely abolished; poverty-stricken areas in western China were gradually exempted from school fees for compulsory education; rural welfare was further developed; and there has been a drive to improve rural roads, water conservancy and all other aspects of rural infrastructure.

During the 4th Session of the 10th National People's Congress held in March 2006, Premier Wen Jiabao met with Chinese and foreign journalists. A reporter asked

A New Chapter on an Old Subject

◆ A park in Xinweizhuang Village in Zhejiang Province surrounded by old-style houses.

him why it is still necessary to concentrate on building a new socialist countryside now when in recent years the central Chinese government has paid great attention to agriculture and to rural areas. Wen answered that this places agriculture and rural areas in a more prominent position in the drive to modernize China as a whole. It is a major step in China's modernization process. Wen's remarks show the overall strategic change in China's development.

Facing Difficult Problems

The goals set for the new countryside certainly paint a wonderful picture: people happy at home and at work, all living a varied, colorful life in beautiful villages.

It is easy to get carried away with this image, but given the myriad rural problems that still have to be resolved and the situation we see in the country right now, people would be forgiven for thinking that, if we are to reach this goal, there is a long and hard journey ahead.

In early 2006, the Chinese news weekly *Outlook* published an article pointing out four major difficulties in building a new countryside:

— The village-level economy is weak. Many villages are unable to fund development, and some of them have run up heavy debts. A new countryside would have to be built without the financial support of village economy.

— Increasing farmers' income will be difficult. Agriculture is vulnerable to market fluctuation and natural disasters so any increase in income is unstable. Farmers are not very market-oriented and there is little competition. Although there is a large number of farmers who work outside their village or migrate, their skill levels are relatively low, so the majority are still engaged in low-income work.

— Rural construction techniques are underdeveloped. The layout of rural houses is disordered and wastes a lot of land. This makes it difficult to develop rural infrastructure. It would be very expensive to modernize the countryside.

— There is no long-term investment plan. Although governments at various administrative levels have intensified their efforts in rural construction, as many villages have outstanding debts, further investment is needed before they can complete their reconstruction. Many local governments obviously cannot reach their targets for reconstruction.

Wang Mengkui, head of the Development Research Center under the State Council, explained the arduousness of the task: "On the one hand, China has a huge population and limited land, and so it is not easy to introduce large-scale agriculture or increase farmers' productivity to any large extent. But to transfer the labor force to non-agricultural industries would be a comparatively long process. On the other hand, China's industry is still only in the development stage itself and will only have limited strength to support agriculture. Even if industrialization and urbanization are progressing smoothly, the rural population will still be over 600 million in 2010 and around 500 million in 2020. Therefore, building a new socialist countryside is a long-term task in the overall drive for modernization and cannot be accomplished all at once."

◆ Bamboo grove in Hongcun Town, Anhui Province.

Faced with so many problems, how should we set about this task? When a large proportion of state funds and all sorts of preferential policies are in place to support rural areas, what is the best way to achieve fast results?

Former Minister of Agriculture Du Qinglin emphasized the importance of developing production, saying that "enhancing the overall productivity of agriculture is the foundation for the building of a new socialist countryside. Without this foundation, the building of a new countryside would be like water without a source or a tree without roots."

Ye Qiwu, a member of the Specialist Council of the Ministry of Construction, emphasized that in the construction process, it is not only necessary to intensify efforts to sustain the countryside through investment and policy, but it is important to put planning first. When it comes to governing villages, if a coherent plan is lacking, then government investment will produce little in the way of positive results and might even have a negative effect.

On the contrary, Professor Wen Tiejun, dean of the Agricultural and Rural Development College of Renmin University, attaches greater importance to the enthusiasm of the farmers. He says, "Investment, no matter how large, is not as good as winning over the farmers. State input should only be used as an initial push to get farmers involved. Only in this way, can the building of a new socialist countryside become a reality."

Professor Lin Yifu, head of the China Center for Economy Research of Peking University, also stressed the human factor: "The new countryside is being built for the farmers, and they will be the main force in its construction. The most important in building a new countryside is that we have open-minded farmers with some know-how for modernization."

There is no simple solution and we cannot expect immediate results. But as people turn their attentions towards the countryside and argue about its development, we are starting to see the vast, unchanging Chinese countryside being reawakened and reinvigorated. In an agricultural history that has already run for several thousand years, this is to be a brand new chapter.

2

How Far Are We from Agricultural Modernization?

In the decades following the founding of New China in 1949, China relied on the development of agriculture to feed the rapidly growing population. The security provided by agricultural production ensured the unimpeded development of the national economy. In looking ahead to the decades to come, population growth and the reduction of arable land means China's grain production problem can no longer be neglected. Now China has entered the international market, its agricultural produce must become more competitive. With a rural population of 800 million, if China is to increase the income of the rural population, it will have to pin its hopes on agriculture.

China has several thousand years of agricultural

◆ A technician testing pesticide residue on vegetables in Shouguang City, Shandong Province.

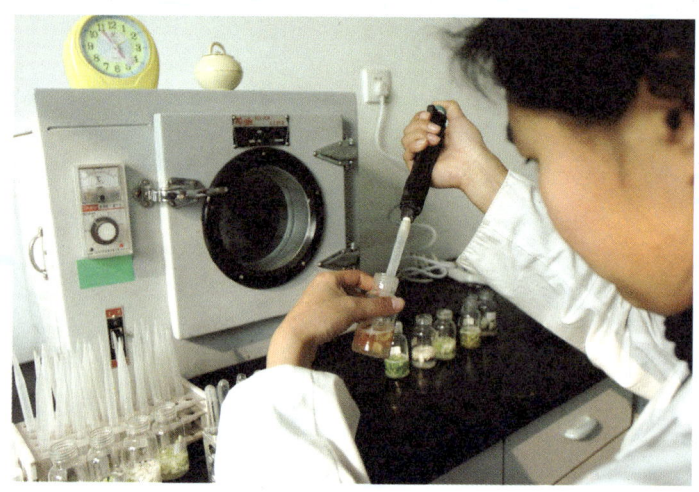

history, but certain problems have caused Chinese agriculture to fall behind that of the United States, Canada and some other developed countries. Some of these problems have been there all along, and others have developed more recently. China has a huge population and little arable land. The growth of the rural population in particular made agricultural resources relatively scarce. The national economy is not yet fully developed, so China is unable to adequately support agriculture. Farmers' have a low level of education, and it will take time to improve this situation. Agricultural infrastructure is poor and farming is not sufficiently scientific or industrialized.

There are many problems to solve before a new countryside can be built.

Water Conservancy: Agriculture's Lifeline

Between 1978 and 1993 China's grain yield leapt from 300 million to 456 million tons. The change from long-term shortage to an aggregate balance to a surplus in good years could not have taken place without the building of numerous irrigation works in the 1970s. These facilities regulate conditions and ensure stable yields even with drought or water-logging.

Today, however, China's agriculture faces a grim reality:

Due to long-term neglect and a lack of management

and maintenance, in many rural areas there exist serious defects in irrigation facilities. Efficiency is low and energy consumption is high. According to statistics from the Ministry of Water Resources, at present in China there are 74 million hectares of farmland that lack irrigation. Of the 56 million hectares of irrigated land, two-thirds continue to use traditional outmoded irrigation methods.

On top of this, water pollution, industry and the development of cities and towns have taken up water that could be used in agriculture. This has led to less water being available for irrigation, an increasing difficulty in finding new water sources for agriculture, and an increase in water charges, with cost per cubic meter standing at above seven yuan.

In some areas in north China it is almost at the stage where all the rivers have dried up and all the water is polluted. Some major rivers and lakes in the south are also polluted in places. The pollution has adversely

◆ A harvester is reaping.

affected the irrigation of crops. In addition, due to the scarcity of water resources, some areas can no longer tap new water sources as underground water has been seriously overexploited.

The importance and urgency of irrigation works have drawn the attention of central and local governments. Since 2004, the State Council has mentioned the irrigation works problem in its main annual report every year for four years.

In the spring of 2007, a model water-saving irrigation project was near completion for over 700 hectares of farmland in Liujiazhuang Town and Yifengdian Town, Jimo City, Shandong Province. It uses a low-pressure piping irrigation system. A network of water pipes is laid under the project area. Vegetables are grown in a large shed and sprinkled with water delivered by the pipes. Some sprays are fixed and others are partially rotating. In the past, despite the two rivers nearby, backward water conservancy facilities and consecutive years of drought meant that crop failure frequently reached emergency levels. Now, improved water conservancy facilities have provided nearby farmlands with sufficient, stable water resources, and advanced irrigation methods have saved water and raised farm yields. It is estimated that the project could save Jimo City 2.016 million yuan in agricultural costs every year. Because of the water conservancy project, many farmers in the area have decided to cultivate vegetables indoor. On average each hectare is now 30 yuan more profitable.

The Jimo City project started in 2006, the same year as the new countryside project was started. That year saw water conservancy projects springing up all round the country. Water conservancy investment from government at all levels increased substantially. The central government's investment was mainly allocated to rural areas and the western provinces. A number of provincial level governments have also substantially increased investment in water conservancy projects.

As small water conservancy facilities had long been in disrepair and there was a serious shortage of maintenance funds, Hunan Province encouraged the people to pool money and labor to deal with the problem. Due to the work of the people and subsidies from the state, the province has effectively accelerated the construction of small water conservancy projects. By the end of October 2006, the province had invested 74.95 million yuan, 89%

of its projected total investment.

Xinjiang Uygur Autonomous Region is committed to water-saving irrigation. By the end of 2006, over 2 million hectares of farmland were benefiting from agricultural water-saving irrigation projects. Highly efficient water-saving technology was available in 560,000 hectares of land, more than anywhere else in the country.

Statistics show that from September 2005 to April 2006, the nation invested a total of 61 billion yuan in basic water conservancy construction, repaired over 270,000 projects that had sustained water damage, heightened and reinforced 20,000 kilometers of dikes, dredged 47,000 kilometers of waterways, de-silted 450,000 kilometers of canals, consolidated over 6,800 small and medium-sized reservoirs, got under control an area of 29,000 sq. km where water was being lost and soil eroded, and built 18,000 projects supplying water to towns and villages that benefit 21 million people.

At the same time, water-saving agriculture has become the most important part of China's water conservancy development. The state is actively improving technology for saving water in farmland, and popularizing fixed quotas of water for use and additional charges on over-used. Where it is possible the use of spray irrigation are expanded, as is the use of sprinklers. Irrigation systems are modified to conserve water. By developing irrigation technology, new projects will introduce water-saving irrigation works to 10 million hectares of farmland within five years. In terms of water conservancy, this will increase the efficiency of irrigation from 45% at present to 50%, whilst simultaneously increasing the total amount of irrigated land. Essentially, there will be no increase in the amount of water used in irrigation.

Figures published by the State Statistics Bureau show that in 2006 the area covered by functional irrigation works had increased by 1.08 million hectares and the area covered by water-saving irrigation works had increased by 1.28 million hectares.

Of course, to make up for the long-term inadequacy of water conservancy construction and fully upgrade irrigation technology, China still has a long way to go. But, no matter how you look at it, China has taken an important first step.

Science and Technology: A New Hope

In the late 1980s, a villager named Wang Leyi in Shouguang County, Shandong Province, used a plastic green house to produce fresh cucumbers and tomatoes in winter, sparking a "white" revolution for China's agriculture in Shandong Province. Since then, growing vegetables in this way has raised the farmers' incomes and Shouguang fast became "The Land of Vegetables." For more than ten years, Shouguang people have

◆ An automatic packing line for milk in Yili Group.

successfully grown vegetables out of season through innovations in science and technology: plastic green houses are constantly being upgraded; thermal insulation is getting better; the cover that keeps vegetables warm at night is now machine operated, drastically reducing labor requirements; carbon dioxide gas fertilizing technology has increased production by 15%; potatoes have been developed that no longer need soil —they are able to grow in water or in air; and tomato "trees" of the height of several people could produce 750 kg of tomatoes a year. Relying on innovation in science and technology, Shouguang's vegetable business leads the country.

However, Shouguang still has technological problems to resolve. On the one hand, over 60% of Shouguang's vegetable seeds were bought at high prices from foreign seed companies. These seeds can only be used once. The seed industry, known as the microchip industry of the agriculture, is becoming the bottleneck hindering the development of Shouguang's vegetable business. On the other hand, in Shouguang's exhibition hall visitors can see all sorts of incredible agricultural innovations, but, due to production cost, many of these innovations are still not widely implemented.

The problems encountered by Shouguang reflect the present typical state of agricultural science and technology in China. In the last few decades China has achieved a remarkable progress in agricultural science and technology: around 48% of Chinese agriculture utilizes new technologies, and in some areas of agricultural science, like super rice and genetically engineered vaccines, China is the world's leader. But in an age when agricultural development is ever more reliant on science and technology, traditional farming techniques are still widely used in China. The role of science and technology played in China is 20-30 lower than it is in developed countries.

During his inspection of a high-tech vegetable gardening area in Shouguang City, Shandong Province, in April 2005, President Hu Jintao said: "The hope of agriculture rests with science and technology." Hu saw that this had been the key to Shouguang's success. Chinese agriculture is weak and must take advantage of these new breakthroughs.

At present, China's investment in agricultural science and technology accounts only for 0.25% of the nation's total agricultural output value, much lower than the world's average of 1%. A report from the Chinese Academy of Agricultural Science showed that, in regard to its contribution to the growth of agricultural output value, the respective return-rate on each yuan invested in education, roads, communication, irrigation and electricity is 3.71, 2.12, 1.91, 1.88 and 0.54 yuan. The return on science and technology is as high as 9.59 yuan.

At the end of 2006, the Ministry of Science and Technology declared that in the next five years, the proportion of fund for scientific research on industry and on agriculture will be changed from 7:3 to 5:5. Moreover, major national science and technology projects and the national science and technology support plan will be focused more on agriculture. For example, under the national science and technology support plan, 3 billion yuan will be allocated to the first batch of agricultural projects during the period of the 11th Five Year Plan (2006-2010). The High-Tech Research and Development Program (the March 1986 Program) will invest 1.4 billion yuan.

The government is also paying attention to raising awareness of agricultural science and technology. At present, Chinese farmers generally have a low level of scientific, technical and cultural knowledge. Their average education is only 7.3 years. Of the 490 million rural workforce, only 13% have received a senior-middle school education or higher. Most farmers continue to use thousand-year-old production techniques. At the same time, as the system for disseminating agricultural technology among ordinary farmers is still ineffective, most innovations in agricultural science languish in laboratories or in a few experimental farms.

Raising awareness of agricultural science and technology is an urgent issue.

In April 2006 when spring sowing was about to start, the Ministry of Agriculture initiated a project to bring agricultural science and technology to households. This project used a pyramid system: experts would guide technical instructors; technical instructors would help set up model households; model households would spread their knowledge to other households. This system had effectively spread fine strains of seeds and scientific farming techniques among ordinary farming households.

This is the second year of the "Technology to the Households" campaign. So far, the Ministry of Agriculture has chosen 212 counties for trial nationwide. Following the pyramid system, provincial authorities have set up a further 389 model counties. The government recruited nearly 5,000 experts for the specialist groups led by the Ministry of Agriculture and

How Far Are We from Agricultural Modernization?

◆ A farmer in Ningxia Hui Autonomous Region showing Chinese wolfberry.

the provincial and county governments, and over 18,000 technical instructors, who trained more than 500,000 model households, with a result that 10 million ordinary farming households have received technical guidance. Statistics show that 90% of those selected as model households in the "Technology to the Households" campaign are either well on their way to using scientific farming techniques or are using them already. In these farms, the grain yield per *mu* (15 *mu* = one hectare) of land is 10% higher than that of ordinary farms, with production costs on average 30 yuan cheaper per *mu*. When talking about the "Technology to the Households" campaign, farmers all say much the same thing: in the past everyone was stuck in their own ways, but now everyone learns from each other.

More and more universities and colleges of agriculture and forestry have joined in with the campaign. Since 2006, the Chinese University of Agriculture has run a program where professors spend time in countryside. Every year, nearly 100 professors from the university go to help in pilot villages. Moreover, teachers become temporary local officials in charge of farming technology and students are encouraged to go to villages and farming households to provide technical support.

Specialized Agriculture

For thousands of years, China's agriculture has been

based on self-sufficiency. The harvest was the only thing that mattered, and what farmers wanted was having enough to eat and to wear. Today, in order for farmers to become better off, agriculture must become a competitive industry.

There is an old Chinese saying that "value lies in rarity." This is the rule that governs the market economy. For agricultural products to become competitive commodities, it is necessary that farmers produce unique goods. China's vast countryside possess abundant natural and cultural resources, and it has been a subject for discussion in countryside as how to use these resources to develop various kinds of special, unique, new or attractive products and relative industries.

The annual China International Agricultural Products Fair was held in Beijing in October 2006. Different from previous years, this year's fair had for the first time set up booths of "One Village, One Product," like Sichuan's "pomegranate village," Shaanxi's "lantern village," Ningxia's "Tanyang sheep village," Shanxi's "millet village," Guizhou's "hot pepper village," Zhejiang's "pearl village" and Yunnan's "Pu'er tea village," attracting many visitors for their exhibits of special and unique local farm products from 35 well-known villages across the country.

Tongkuang Village of Huili County, Sichuan Province, was one of the exhibitors at the fair, which had 98% of its total agricultural output value from the pomegranate industry. The per-capita income from its pomegranate industry was 7,279 yuan in 2005, accounting for 98.6% of the net income of each villager. Tanshan Village of Qinxian County, Shanxi Province, has a population of 218 people, and its income in 2005 from millet production was 3.4 million yuan, 60% of the village's total income. In Xiazi Village of Zunyi County, Guizhou Province, its processing of chili pepper brings nearly 10 million yuan to the village every year. Dazhigou Village of Zunhua City, Hebei Province, was known as the "Land of Chestnuts," and each villager could earn 4,000 yuan from chestnut production every year. In Sanzhao Village of Xi'an, Shaanxi Province, known as the "Town of Lanterns," 980 farming households are engaged in the making of lanterns, accounting for 90% of the total households.

The main goal of the Ministry of Agriculture's "One Village, One Product" strategy is that Chinese agriculture will move towards large-scale, standardized, market-oriented production of fruits, vegetables, livestock, forestry and other produces. In the end a production pattern will gradually be formed that each county has its main economic sector, each township has its main industry, each village has its special projects, and each household has its products. The Ministry is adopting measures to support the development of a host of industries. Many local governments have set up special agriculture development funds to encourage villages to develop their own specialized industries.

In order to build a new countryside, rural non-material industries are also developing rapidly. Rural tourism is a good example. Statistics show that at present, the nation has 359 model agricultural tourist destinations established following the initiative of the State Tourism Administrative Administration. They are scattered across 31 provinces, autonomous regions and municipalities. They are engaged in many different types of agricultural fields including farming, forestry, animal husbandry, sideline occupations, fishery, crop cultivation, fish breeding, poultry raising, and processing. 2006 was designated as China's "Year of Rural Tourism" by the State Tourism Administration. Its slogan was "new agriculture, new tourism and new experience."

The administration's idea has promoted the development of rural tourist industry. Rural areas in Wuyuan County, Jiangxi Province, known as the most beautiful countryside in China, have attracted large numbers of tourists in recent years. In 2006, the State Tourism Administration helped Wuyuan County to start rural tourism, and the county received 2.83 million tourists and had an total income of 470 million yuan.

"One Village, One Product" and rural tourism reflect

◆ A farmer in Ningxia Hui Autonomous Region displaying a cabbage introduced from Switzerland.

the changes that have been made to the country's agricultural sector and the big transformation of rural products. By 2006, the state had marked out 41 advanced production areas, including those producing main agricultural goods.

Besides developing specialized agriculture, improving quality is making Chinese agricultural goods more competitive. Chinese agriculture has a long tradition of intensive cultivation. Experts think that intensive cultivation can not only solve the problem of the rural labor surplus, but can also increase rural incomes if it produces green food.

Beijing's Pinggu District is a peach-growing area.

It has more than 40 peach varieties, planted in an area of 15,000 hectares, producing 200 million kilograms of peaches a year. At present 7,000 hectares have been awarded the state's quality standards certification, over 333 hectares the state's organic food accreditation, and 3,000 hectares the state's green food authentication. Due to their safe and standardized production, Pinggu's peaches are not only selling well on the home market, but are also exported to Southeast Asia and Europe, bringing 40,000 households of peach growers an annually increased income of 8,000 yuan on average.

At the same time many rural areas are trying to get farmers more involved in the processing, packaging and sales of agricultural produces so that farmers are able to share the profits beyond farming.

Xingshisi Village of Heilongjiang Province used to grow corn as its main crop. Since it began to get involved in the processing of corn, the village has become more prosperous and is now known as the "No.1 Village of Heilongjiang." As the village's Party secretary Fu Huating said, "You'll never get rich just by growing corn. At the beginning, Xingshisi Village used good seeds, bought large farm machines, and introduced water-saving irrigation and many other techniques. The production went up and farmers' income was increased, but it was a slow progress. This money could help improve people's lives but was far from enough to develop production. Later when the village started the processing of farm products, things were much improved. Take corn, for example, now its market price is high— one ton of corn can sell for 1,000 yuan. But processed corn can sell at more than 10,000 yuan per ton, 10 times more than what we made previously. The processed JPC biological health corn sells at 50 yuan a bottle. There isn't any competition on the market for it yet, so we're able to sell as many as we produce." Now the average per-capita income of Xingshisi Village has reached 20,000 yuan.

The development of villages like those in Wuyuan County, Pinggu District and Xingshisi Village has given rural China new confidence. As long as markets and products are thoroughly investigated, industrialized agricultural management can be expanded and improved.

Some problems, though, are unavoidable. A village is not an enterprise. If each farming household were going its own way, it would be impossible for them to unite and, as a whole, to set up an industrialized agriculture.

Reforming Cooperatives

Xiaogang Village, Fengyang County, Anhui Province, is a household name in China. In 1978, when Chinese rural areas were still engaged in collectivized production, villagers of 18 households in Xiaogang Village risked applying to divide their collective farmlands and went it alone. This move anticipated the later rural reforms. In 2006, the year marking the beginning of the "Building a New Countryside" project, Xiaogang Village organized cooperatives based on a new model and went down the road of collectivization once more.

After the villagers applied to divide their land, they quickly escaped poverty and food and clothing were no longer a problem. But things did not continue to improve at such a rate. There was a shortage of land, and the land was anyway of poor quality. On top of that, traffic links were not good and there was a shortage of labor. This made it difficult for households in Xiaogang Village to make any more great leaps if they continued to rely on individual farming. So, on February 18, 2006, Party secretary Shen Hao of Xiaogang Village called a meeting and asked the whole village their opinions on land management. At the meeting, Shen Hao announced that for Xiaogang Village to develop cooperatives, farmers' land would be rented at 33.3 yuan per hectare, and, for every hectare planted with wheat, an extra 20 yuan fee would be levied to buy young crop. Shen Hao outlined the need for Xiaogang Village to change from the previous practice of farming on a household basis to the development of cooperatives on a unified leaseback contract. Shen Hao said that they should collectivize the land to take advantage of all their resources, and their focus should be on the development of industrialized agriculture.

Xiaogang is not the first village to reconstruct cooperatives. In recent years, many farmers' specialized economic cooperatives have emerged in rural areas across China.

Last century when China's agriculture changed from collectivized production to individual production, farmers were undoubtedly reinvigorated. However, as farmers chased further development in agriculture, it became clear that small-scale production on a household basis could only be stretched so far. Farming households are unstable and, when they run into difficulties, they are too weak to protect themselves. No single person can control floods, droughts or bad harvests. No single person can meet market challenges and protect themselves against others infringing on their interests.

With this in mind many farmers decided to once again pool their funds and wisdom and work together. Arm in arm they would pursue new avenues of development. Since farming households are engaged in the same industry, encounter similar difficulties, use similar specialized techniques and materials and produce goods for the same market, they have the same needs in the production process. When farmers unite, service is more efficient as it is on a large scale, it encourages farmers to specialize by dividing labor, it can effectively

◆ Farmers in Mengcheng County in Anhui Province selecting tractors in the market to prepare for the coming agriculture season.

reduce the cost of production and sales, and effectively provide a link between the small-scale production of thousands of households and the ever-changing market.

Yutan Village in Rudong County, Jiangsu Province, has traditionally specialized in cotton production. It unified its layout, the variety of cotton produced, auxiliary technology and purchases. Its cotton yield increased nearly 20% in three years and its cotton cultivation efficiency significantly increased.

The reason why the industrial methods of the aforementioned Xingshisi Village were so successful is that they relied on large-scale, united production. At first, there were many factories in the village, but all of them produced on a small scale and had few prospects. Later, the village used the funds it had accumulated over the years to modify existing enterprises for large-scale industry, organize them into groups, and develop more than 30 products that it divides into four categories: biological products, fine chemicals, health products, and fodder. The corn processing chain is the longest in the country. Its corn beer, JPC health products and JPC fodder have all filled gaps on home market and hold a leading position on international market.

Following the beginning of the "Building a New Countryside" project, various kinds of cooperative organizations have sprung up across China. Due to the many difficulties encountered by farmers' cooperatives in gaining official recognition and guaranteeing funds, the Chinese government has adopted many measures to protect these incipient organizations which are helping to increase farmers' income.

On July 6, 2006, a study group was convened in Beijing for city and provincial level cadres who are involved in agriculture. The subject to be discussed was "Building a New Socialist Countryside Through Developing Specialization, Cooperation and the Rural Economy." Yin Chengjie, the vice-minister of agriculture, said that encouraging and guiding farmers to develop organizations in these three areas is a major step in the building of a new socialist countryside

On October 31, 2006, the "Law on Farmers' Specialized Cooperatives" was passed by the Standing Committee of the National People's Congress, which provides a legal guarantee for cooperatives looking to break into the market. To strengthen support for cooperatives, the Law has a section specifically on supportive policy. This section clearly stipulates that the state supports development of agricultural and rural economic construction projects and that qualified farmers' specialized cooperatives can be entrusted with the implementation of these projects. Central and local treasuries should both arrange funding and support farmers' specialized cooperatives in setting up new services in areas like information, training, quality stan-

◆ Huangyangtan Farm in Ningxia Hui Autonomous Region has installed international advanced power-driven circular spay irrigation system.

dards and product approval, the construction of infrastructure for agricultural production, spreading marketing techniques and technology. Priority is to be given to specialized cooperatives in ethnic minority regions, remote border regions and poverty-stricken regions, and to cooperatives which produce urgently needed agricultural products.

Government Support

As farmers unite and produce specialized products on a large scale, the government is there to help smooth the process of taking the products from the countryside into the market. It acts as a guide to specialized industries, offering advice on such difficult problems as funding, technology, marketing and branding.

In the first few years when Sichuan's Huili County was turning itself into the "land of pomegranates," the county treasury invested over 2 million yuan every year to help pay for publicity alone. It paid for exhibitions, advertising, trademarks registration, and applications for the protection of the area which originally produced the pomegranates. In addition, to help the pomegranate industry, the county encouraged investment from other sources, organized exhibitions, standardized cultivation, trained farmers, supported production, and helped farmers solve problems they encountered in developing the industry which they could not solve themselves. The county has been rewarded for its efforts. It has built 30 specialized pomegranate villages, runs a specialized wholesale market and owns several leading enterprises engaging in the processing of fruit, juice, and fruit wine. Huili's pomegranates are known far and wide and have a firm foothold in the market. The pomegranate industry's contribution to local tax revenue is growing by 15% per year.

In 1983 a cold wave in Shouguang County, Shandong, left huge amounts of cabbage rotting in the field and made it completely unsalable. Ever since, the city government has begun to devote a great deal of energy to building a vegetable wholesale market. Now Shouguang's vegetable growers have one of northern China's very best vegetable wholesale markets and farmers no longer worry about being unable to sell their vegetables.

Xiazi Village, Xiazi Town, Zunyi City, Guizhou Province, has been producing chili pepper for a long time. When the powerful "Mom's" food group set up shop in Xiazi Town, the chili pepper industry quickly spread through the whole town. The town council secretary for political and legal affairs, Liang Zhong, told reporters that with the impetus provided by Xiazi Village and "Mom's," the town has more than 5,000 people directly involved with the pepper industry and the urban population has risen sharply from 3,000 to 15,000 people.

Developing Modern Agriculture

In 2006, China's grain yield surpassed 490 million tons. It was the first time since 1985 that China's grain

◆ Farmers cultivating flowers in greenhouse.

yield had increased for three years continuously. The per-capita income of villagers reached 3,587 yuan a year. It was also the first time in twenty years that farmers' incomes had raised by over 6% a year for three years in a row.

At the Central Rural Work Conference held at the end of 2006, Vice-premier Hui Liangyu said that the primary task in advancing the construction of a new countryside is modernizing agriculture. In the future, although the agriculture's proportional contribution to the GDP will gradually decline, agriculture's role as the foundation of the national economy and its strategic significance will not change and, in fact, will become more important.

In the No. 1 document of 2007 of the Central Government, countryside still remains the main theme. The document insists that modernizing agriculture is

the main task in building a new socialist countryside. Promoting the construction of modern agriculture is fundamental to increasing farmers' income and to making agriculture more productive. It is the base for building a new socialist countryside. For agricultural progress it must have modern materials, modern science and technology, a modern industrial system, modern management techniques, and a modern concept of development. It is necessary to train new-style farmers, and raise the level of agricultural water conservancy

◆ Returning home from shool.

works, machinery and communications.

In 2007, the Central Treasury allocated 500 million yuan to help spread agricultural technology, 900 million yuan to subsidize experimental programs and support the development of land-specific fertilizer, 300 million yuan to subsidize the development of agricultural industrialization and the processing industry, 11.5 billion yuan to the overall development of agriculture, focusing on improving the productivity and efficiency of agriculture, and 1.1 billion yuan to train farmers with scientific techniques and those who need to possess new skills for reemployment.

At the 1st Session of the 1st National People's Congress held in 1954, Premier Zhou Enlai announced for the first time the magnificent plan to achieve the "four modernizations." The modernization of agriculture was one of the four. China has strived to realize that goal for half a century. Whether it is "modernization of agriculture" as in 1954, the "development of production" as in the plan to build a new countryside, or "modern agriculture" as it is today, the underlying idea has never changed: to make Chinese agriculture a formidable force.

3

A New Look for Ancient Villages

*Some houses dotted here and there
And even the odd thatched cottage,
Eaves under elm and willow umbrage
Before the hall stand the peach and pair.*

*Villages sit distant and sunny,
Ruins in an undulating haze.*

◆ Nineteen pairs of brides and bridegrooms, who are vegetable growers, holding a collective wedding ceremony in Shouguang City, the birthplace of greenhouse vegetables in Shandong Province.

Dogs' barks are lost in the lanes' maze,
Hens cluck by the mulberry tree.

The courtyards clean, empty and bare,
Inside the walls there is not a care.

This poem by Tao Yuanming (372-427) vividly depicts a quiet and delightful village. Today, there are still many beautiful scenes to be found in China's vast countryside. With their enchanting scenery these are ideal places for tourism. However, leaving aside the countryside found in poems and tourist brochures, what does the countryside inhabited by the majority of farmers really look like? This is a question that can only be answered by actually going deep into ordinary villages.

Rural infrastructure and public services can seem insufficient and discordant when compared with urban areas, where they are fairly complete. The problems are very noticeable: residential areas are often dirty, disordered and of poor quality, there is no road access and the water supply is unhygienic. Even in some economically developed rural areas, infrastructure and public services are still seriously sub-standard. Farmers might have houses and cars, but there is still not a decent toilet.

Improving the environment in rural residential areas and perfecting public facilities is, therefore, an important step on the road to urbanization and modernization. Improving the rural environment is one of the main goals in building a new socialist countryside. In 2006 the primary report of the Central Government clearly states that building up rural infrastructure is an important task. It calls for efforts to strengthen the infrastructure most needed in farmers' daily life, improve village planning and improve people's living environment.

Construction of Infrastructure

In the initial rush of enthusiasm to build a new countryside, some places took "improving the rural environment" to mean "making the countryside tidy and beautiful." They set up about large-scale demolition projects in order to rebuild villages from scratch. "New" was the only thing that mattered. This not only wasted huge amounts of money and resources, it often produced negative results as it ran counter to farmers' wishes and even added to their burden.

The state's financial resources are limited. There are many areas whose living environment needs improving but there is no way for everywhere to advance at the same rate. It is impossible to complete all villages and all projects at one fell swoop, and still less possible to pull everything down and rebuild. With limited financial resources, we can only work on a village by village basis. Starting with the most urgently needed infrastructure, it is necessary to improve rural living conditions in a way that wastes a minimum of capital and resources and that does not add to the burden of farmers.

If we look at funds allocated to supporting the construction of rural infrastructure in recent years, especially since the start of the construction of a new countryside, we can see that these funds were mainly used in road, water conservancy and methane projects.

Road Construction. It is a very popular saying in China that if you want to get rich, you must first build

◆ A bus traveling on the newly-built road, which connects villages with Pingyang County, Shandong Province.

♦ Senior citizens in Wanglanzhuang Village in Tianjin Municipality chatting on the square nearby their houses.

roads. Since 2003, the Ministry of Communications has made major changes to its plan for road construction, intensifying its efforts and increasing its funding. By the end of 2005, the percentage of the country's townships and towns and administrative villages with roads running to them reached 99.8% and 94.5% respectively. Ten provinces had asphalt roads to every township, and three provinces had asphalt roads to every village.

Some statistics, though, present a very different picture of rural roads. At the end of 2005, in the five autonomous regions (Inner Mongolia, Guangxi, Tibet, Ningxia and Xinjiang) and four provinces (Yunnan, Guizhou, Qinghai and Sichuan) there were 16,000 administrative villages with no road links. Many natural villages simply had no roads at all. Whenever it is windy, clouds of dust are stirred up; whenever it rains, it gets terribly muddy. Even townships sometimes have rough and bumpy roads that are very difficult for cars. There is no way for villagers to conveniently transport their farm produces, and purchasers are unwilling to go to these villages to buy directly. This made it very difficult for the village to develop.

In 2006, the Ministry of Communications declared that in the next five years, the ministry will implement a "100-Billion-Yuan Road Construction Project in Five Years." Emphasis will be put on improving rural road construction, and building and rebuilding 1.2 million kilometers of rural road, so that, where conditions allow, all Chinese towns and townships and natural villages will have access to roads, and 95% of townships and towns and 80% of administrative villages will have access to asphalt (cement) roads.

Improving Water Quality. Water is the source of life. However, it is not rare that one hears sayings like "one street, two rows of houses, and a stinking pond at the back." This actually describes the real water situation in some regions. Many villages are faced with such problems as drinking water being contaminated, carrying snail fever, or containing high levels of fluorine (F), arsenic (As), or salt. Some regions have insufficient drinking water.

Although between 2000 and 2004 the state spent over 20 billion yuan improving the drinking water situation for 60 million people living in rural areas, by the end of 2004 there were still 323 million rural people without safe drinking water, about 34% of the total rural population.

In 2006, the Central Government spent a total of 6 billion yuan, and local governments spent 6.9 billion yuan on providing people with access to drinking water and on making sure that water is safe. The Ministry of

◆ Kids in Panyang Village in Guangxi Zhuang Autonomous Region are curious about the newly-installed telephone.

Water Resources predicts that in the next five years its priority will be to provide safe drinking water for 100 million rural people. In August that same year, the State Council raised the target to 160 million rural people and decided that within 10 years (that is by 2015) they would aim to effectively solve the drinking water problem for 300 million rural people.

New Energy Sources. In recent years, in order to solve rural environment and fuel problems, China has begun to energetically implement the marsh gas project in rural areas. In this project, various pollutants are sent to methane-generating pits to be reused. As a result of this incipient project, farmers will be able to leave behind many traditional and backward living habits. In many villages methane construction is being combined with the rebuilding of toilets, kitchens, and sheepfolds and pigsties. With methane farmers no longer need to struggle with smoke and fire when cooking. Toilets, sheepfolds and pigsties will become clean and hygienic—not the dirty, smelly places they once were. In due course family courtyards and the village as a whole will become neat and tidy. Moreover, the methane project will improve the efficiency of fuel and fertilizer and this will help farming households economize and increase their income.

By the end of 2005, over 18 million farming households were using marsh gas and 7 billion cubic meters of methane were being produced every year, the equivalent of 5.24 million tons of standard coal. The living conditions of more than 50 million rural residents suffering energy shortages were improved through the use of clean gas fuel. By 2010, it is hoped that 40 million rural households will be using marsh gas, with 28.4% of households capable of introducing the project. Great effort will made to push that figure up to 70% by the year 2020, essentially universalizing the use of rural marsh gas.

In 2006 the country rebuilt 325,000 kilometers of rural highways and nearly 20,000 administrative villages were running scheduled passenger buses, unprecedented in terms of investment and the distance of rural roads completed. On top of that, 28.97 million people living in rural areas were provided with safe drinking water, and around 4.5 million more households started using methane. Farmers' lives are being improved step by step by drainage ditches, garbage dumping yards, disaster-prevention facilities, public fire-fighting equipment and a number of other improvements to rural infrastructure. Many of these things are appearing in the countryside for the very first time.

The Importance of Scientific Planning

The benefit of the "Improving the Rural Environment" project will be seen more quickly than the "Development of Production" project or the "Higher Income" project. Because of this some people think that, as long as there is state financial support, rural construction and changing the appearance of the countryside will be easy. But it is not as simple as one might imagine.

Because the drinking water of a certain village contained colibacillus, the government offered money to dig a new well. But the new well was dug less than 10 meters away from the old one. Cow dung, human excreta and the village sewage that affected the water quality of the old well are in close proximity to the new well. Obviously it won't be long until the problems of the old well will start to affect the new well. If a plan had been worked out in accordance with town planning standards, the new well would have been built to the windward side of the residential area.

There is a mountain village which built a cement road in the course of the reconstruction of its highways. Before long, the villagers discovered that on rainy days, mud would cover the road. Animals could easily slip and fall when walking on the road, and so it was very dangerous. Villagers then used chisels to form rough ruts on the muddy road surface to prevent skidding. Villagers realized the cement road should not have been built at that time. Instead the road should have been built with sand and stones, and the money thus saved

◆ Private car in use.

could have been used to widen other roads.

These two stories tell us that before investing in village construction, it is necessary to draw up a scientific and coherent plan. If construction is pursued blindly, government investment will bear no results and might even have a negative effect.

There are also some places which adopt the simplistic "demolition and reconstruction" method. This not only wastes funds, but would result in villages losing their unique characteristics. Many experts are deeply concerned about this. One expert remarks, "That wouldn't be 'construction,' it would be the 'destruction' of rural civilization. What we need is to build villages with Chinese characteristics, not simply 'Western-style' buildings in some pursuit of uniformity. Rural construction is not simply replacing the old with the new; rather the goal is to plan, on any given scale, a natural and unique historical and cultural space."

This is a very complicated and pains-taking work. In the planning process, we must act according to the

◆ A girl in Sanxi Town of Sichuan Province chatting on line with her parents, who are migrant workers in a big city.

local conditions, and examine the nature and details of a certain village as well as the particulars of its ecosystem. Then follow-up examinations must be made to deduce the environmental influence of existing and upcoming projects, eliminate any dangers that might affect the village's security, protect rural residents' ecological and residential environment, and try to save construction costs where possible.

With the launch of the new countryside project, the importance of planning is being gradually understood by more and more localities. Many experts have begun to take part in the planning of village construction. They are building a new countryside through inspection of the area and detailed talks with villagers. They are then able to adopt the most scientific, rational and economical methods.

4

Blue Skies over City and Country

The Road to a New Countryside

A farmer is someone who tills the fields. This is a universally recognized definition. But in China, a "farmer" has long been seen as more of an identity than a profession.

In the early 1950s, when New China had just been founded, there was a lot to be done. It was decided that urban industrialization was the basis for the economy if China were to build it into a powerful country. Following this decision the Chinese economy developed rapidly. However, the continual increase in the number of factory workers increased the pressure on cities. As a result, China was short of food supply.

Although the low level of agricultural production was the main reason for the food shortage, the huge numbers of farmers pouring into the cities was also an important factor. In order to guarantee the state's food security, China began the division of residence permits

◆ Parents bringing kids back home from the kindergarten in Qiaoshan Village of Fujian Province, which is free to farmers.

for urban and rural areas. It was stipulated that farmers would be obliged to sell grain to the state and that rationing would be implemented in urban areas. It was because of this situation New China's permanent residence system took shape.

Given China's circumstances at that time, the residence system was absolutely necessary. If the policy hadn't been adopted, it would have been very difficult to effectively limit the flow of the enormous rural population into the cities or to guarantee the food supply of the cities. Later, however, too many things were reliant on the residence system. Medical security, good-quality education and social welfare were all more readily available in cities and towns. As a result, the development of rural education, culture, health care, social insurance and other public services lagged behind for a long time. In many aspects, farmers basically had to look after themselves.

In 2004, 77% of the nation's public education budget and over 80% of its public medical and health services budget was spent on cities. The ratio of social security coverage between urban and rural areas was 22:1.

The system whereby the city supports the countryside economically and the countryside provides food for the city has been the foundation of China's development. The "Building a New Countryside" has shifted that focus. It aims to change the system whereby residence permits make the country and city two different worlds. China's 800 million farmers have already pinned their hopes on this policy and the Chinese government is devoting its attention to it.

Improving Education

In recent years education has become the biggest expense for many rural families. A survey revealed that from October 2004 to October 2005, rural families with children at school were spending 32.6% of their family income on their children's education. In rural areas, it is difficult for ordinary families to cope with the education fees of their children, and so there are many rural children who are forced to leave school. The result is that the average rural laborer has only received about seven years of schooling.

The problem of rural education facilities is equally serious. In many rural areas, especially in the central and western regions, school buildings, desks and teaching facilities are very simple— even the most basic teaching conditions are not available. Eighty percent of the school houses in the nation's primary and middle schools which are classed as dilapidated are in rural areas. Two-thirds of all students live in rural areas, but urban schools have two-thirds of the computers. Rural teachers are often not paid regularly.

If rural youths are outside the age bracket for compulsory education, and thus fail to receive their nine-year compulsory education, or if the quality of education is very low, for years to come, it will be difficult from them to improve their cultural level. Although vocational training can help, even it requires a basic level of education to be effective. If illiteracy and semi-illiteracy become common among youths and adults then, like a period of rapid population growth, the country will have serious negative effects in its future. Therefore when China's education system is reformed, and compulsory education gradually becomes free, rural education will be a priority.

In 2006, the Chinese government declared that in two years students in rural schools of compulsory education would be exempt from tuition and other school fees. Besides this exemption, the government will also provide free textbooks for students with financial difficulties and will subsidize the living costs of poor students who return to school. This policy is called the "Two Exemptions and One Subsidy." Because the cost of education has been reduced by several hundred yuan, many rural children are desperate to go to school and pursue their dreams. For farmers, this is as welcome as the exemption from agricultural tax.

In his "Work Report of the Government" delivered at the 4th Session of the 10th National People's Congress held on March 5, 2006, Premier Wen Jiabao declared that in the next five years the treasury will spend an extra 218.2 billion yuan on compulsory education. The money will mainly be used to supplement public funds for compulsory education in rural primary and middle schools, to fund the maintenance and renovation of rural primary and middle school buildings, and guarantee the salary for rural primary and middle school teachers.

As for higher education, poor university students are also receiving more and more attention. Chinese college entrance examinees and university students come largely from rural areas and their families' income mostly from farming crops or from migrant work in cities. Take Qinghai Province for example, the annual net income of poor farmers is below 800 yuan, but since 1994, Chinese university tuition has risen from several hundred yuan to 5,000-8,000 yuan a year. Students studying in colleges or universities in Qinghai have to pay for tuition, living costs and other expenses totaling around 10,000 yuan a year. To support an undergraduate a family would need at least 40,000 yuan, which would take a poor farmer 50 years to earn.

In 2006, the "Investigation into Poverty Stricken Chinese College Entrance Examinees" carried out by the China Youth Development Trust found that, of the college entrance examinees surveyed, 59.9% said they could not cover the costs of their first year tuition fee and 12.7% students gave up their dream of entering university because of the excessive economic burden that would be placed on their families. For the overwhelming majority of poor students, even if they were admitted to universities, their family economic difficulties would greatly affect their daily life including food, clothing, housing and transportation and studies, causing physical and mental stress on them.

"We won't let a single university student drop out because of poverty" — that was the goal set by the Ministry of Education. To realize this goal, the ministry called on institutions of higher education to set up a

◆ A view of an old people's home completed in 2006 in Pingyuan County, Shandong Province.

"green passage" system at the beginning of every semester. Once new students have taken care of matriculation formalities, if they have financial difficulties, they will be offered means-tested financial-aid to ensure their study. On no condition is a university or college allowed to refuse to admit a student because of their financial difficulties.

In order to help children from families with financial difficulties or from low-income families to complete their higher education, China has set up a system of grants. This includes the state grant and scholarship program, the work-study program, and special difficulty subsidy program. Since the implementation of the state grant and loan system in 1999, 2.405 million students have been granted state subsidies or loans by the end of June 2006, with a total of 20.14 billion yuan being transferred to students from banks.

A New-Style Rural Cooperative Medical System

Two years ago, if you asked farmers the question, "What are you most worried about?" many of them would answer, "I'm afraid of getting sick."

In recent years, medical expenses have been rising continually. Even urbanites who have medical insurance are struggling. For farmers without insurance, the cost of medical treatment and prescriptions can be too much for them to bear. An immediate result of the lack of a rural medical insurance is that farmers' standard of health has not improved and may even have declined. The numbers of rural people who are made poor or who fall back into poverty because of illness is increasing with each passing day, canceling out government efforts to reduce poverty. Statistics show that in recent years, more than 10 million rural people a year on average sink into poverty or return to poverty, greatly reducing the effect of any efforts to help the poor.

At one point in the 1960s and 1970s, 90% of the nation's rural population was covered by the rural cooperative medical system. A cooperative medical system, rural health stations and a huge number of barefoot doctors were the three magic weapons for solving the lack of trained doctors and medicine in China's rural areas. The system was praised by the World Bank and World Health Organization (WHO) as the only example of a developing country being able to solve the problem of medical expenses. But after the 1980s, due to the downsizing of the collective economy, the rural cooperative medical service lost its economic footing and so was discontinued.

To alleviate this problem, in 2003, a new-style rural cooperative medical system was launched on an experimental basis in some counties and county-level cities. Under the system towns are usually organized by households. Each person makes a voluntary contribu-

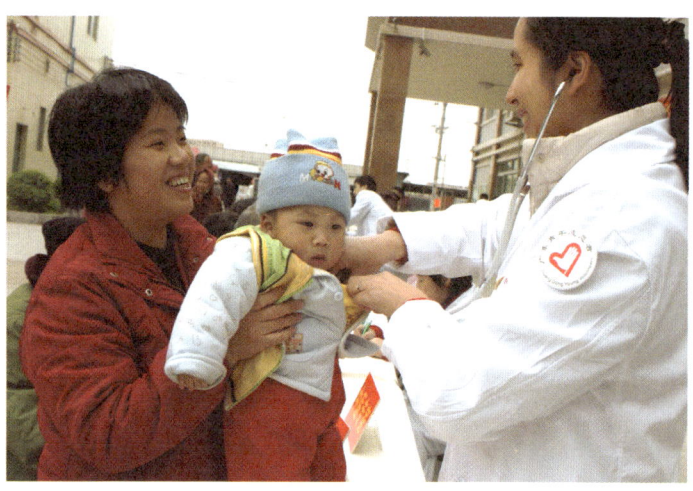

◆ Doctors from Guangzhou No.1 People's Hospital doing free health checkup for kids in Shiling Town, Guangdong Province.

tion of no less than 10 yuan a year into the cooperative medical fund. The local government offers a subsidy of no less than 20 yuan per person. The Central Government offers an additional subsidy of no less than 20 yuan to farmers in the central and western regions participating in the scheme. Together these three contributions make up the rural cooperative medical fund. In addition, the government has set up a special bank account to pay out reimbursements. In the event of being hospitalized, farmers participating in the cooperative medical system are entitled to be reimbursed for a proportion of their medical expenses.

By the end of 2006, around 400 million farmers were already covered by the new-style rural cooperative medical system. Although the amount raised in funds and paid out in reimbursements is not high, for the first time in history, through government support, about three quarters of China's rural population are able to obtain extra financial support when they go to the doctor. In 2007, the treasury earmarked 10.1 billion yuan to pay for subsidies, 5.8 billion yuan more than the previous year. From an experimental project the system has been

◆ Zhang Haiqiang, a doctor in Zhonghe Town in Ningxia Hui Autonomous Region, introducing the New Village Cooperative Medical Treatment System to a villager.

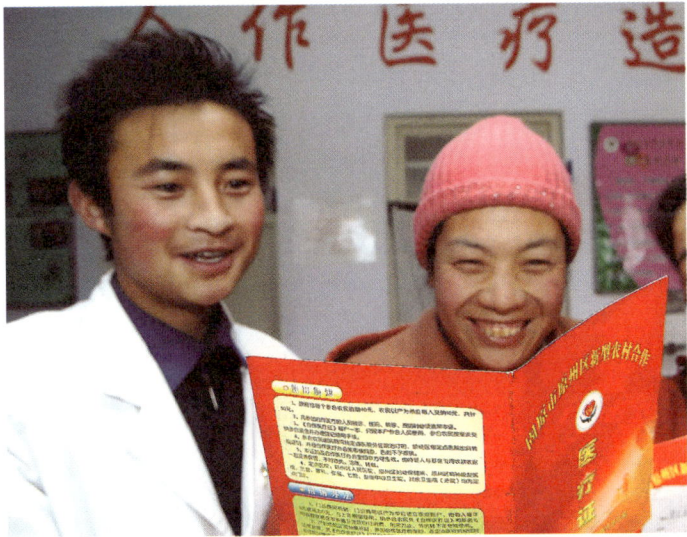

◆ Pupils cleaning desks in their new classroom in Xiushan Primary School, the first one constructed under the Invigorating Village Education Plan implemented by Shizhong District in Jinan City, Shandong Province.

expanded to over 80% of the nation's counties and county-level cities.

Villager He Xianmi has a family of five in Yili Village, Jinzhong Town, Huize County, Yunnan Province. The family has an annual income of 2,000-3,000 yuan from growing two *mu* (15mu=one hectare) of tobacco. In early 2006, the family joined the new cooperative medical system. In June, He's son had a surgery costing over 1,300 yuan. After he was discharged from hospital, he immediately went into town where he was reimbursed for 45% of his medical expenses. With 590 yuan of cash in hand, He's wife was full of praise for the new cooperative medical system. She said that every penny counts for farmers and the 590 yuan is a big deal. It is equivalent of 20 bags of chemical fertilizer and seven piglets!

"That's something that could never have been done under the old cooperative medical system," said, emotionally, a leading grassroots cadre working with the health department when he talked about the benefit to farmers brought by the new medical system. The new cooperative medical system is now in operation. What is new is that the government and farmers jointly raise money for the farmers' medical expenses, and the government contributing the larger portion while farmers contributing the smaller.

In his Government Work Report delivered at the 4th Session of the 10th National People's Congress, Premier Wen Jiabao pointed out that the underdeveloped medical and health service in China's rural areas cannot completely satisfy farmers' basic needs. This has become a serious problem for China's current economic and social development. He called on governments at all levels to place the accelerated development of rural health services high on their agenda and said it should be considered an important task in the building of a new socialist countryside. In his report he promised that, by 2008, the cooperative medical system would cover all rural areas and, by 2010, a rural health service network with relatively complete basic facilities would be in the early stages of construction. By that time every farmer will be able to enjoy basic health services.

Minimal Living Security System

Statistics show that in 2003 China's GDP (gross domestic product) grew 9.1% over the previous year, the fastest period of growth since 1997. It was the first time that the per-capita GDP exceeded US$1,000. But some statistics were not so positive. In 2003, the population of China's rural abject poor, instead of decreasing, increased by 800,000 people.

In the year 2005, the number of the abject poor in China's rural areas stood at 23.65 million, and the population in low-income groups came to 40.67 million. This indicates that economic growth had not brought benefit to the poorest members of society. Residents in urban families with a per-capita income lower than the poverty line are entitled to government's minimal living allowance, but what about farmers?

Since 1997, some Chinese provinces and cities, where conditions allow, have begun to gradually set up a rural minimal living security system. Guangdong, Zhejiang and other economically developed regions have each implemented the "Rural Minimal Living Security Plan", extending social security to include farmers. By the end of 2006, 24 provinces nationwide had begun setting up rural minimal living security systems, which will benefit more than 13 million people.

However, in many less developed regions, local governments have financial difficulties and are often unable to provide adequate financial support for a rural minimal living allowance. Likewise, the rural collective economy is weak and finds it hard to allocate a large amount of money to support rural minimal living

◆ Pupils in Dupeng Village in Guizhou Province practicing typing with a re-equipped black-and-white television as a computer.

security system. In fact, in places like these there are more people living in poverty, affecting the ability of the region to establish a rural minimal living security system.

In December 2006, the Central Rural Work Conference stated for the first time that active efforts would be made to explore ways to establish a social security system that would cover urban and rural residents, and to establish a rural minimal living security system throughout the country. Earlier at the National Financial Work Conference in 2006, Finance Minister Jin Renqing indicated that in 2007 the treasury would increase funds to popularize the establishment of the rural minimal living security system. This suggests that the treasury will strongly support the establishment of a rural minimal living security system.

In 2007, the treasury earmarked 3 billion yuan to subsidize rural minimal living allowances. This will encourage regions that have set up this system to further improve it and encourage regions that do not have this system to set it up as soon as possible. In March 2007, Vice-Minister Li Liguo of Civil Affairs declared that the rural minimal living security system was expected to be completed in the first half of the year and benefit millions of rural people.

5

Farmers Hang up Their Farm Tools

◆ Workers busy with their work in a carpet factory in Xinjiang Uyghur Autonomous Region.

"You till land while I weave; you fetch water while I water the garden." A rural life like this, lived in harmony with the rest of the world, has been the aspiration of Chinese farmers for thousand years. Spring plowing and autumn harvesting, the cycle of the four seasons: that used to be what Chinese farmers had to worry about. Today, however, this situation is undergoing tremendous changes: land is no longer the only thing on which farmers depend for subsistence and the countryside is no longer the only place farmers spend their whole life. Many Chinese farmers have hung up their farm tools and are starting to look for other jobs outside their farm land.

There are many complicated reasons why farmers leave their land:

— The population is growing, but arable land is decreasing. Farming techniques are developing, so agricultural production is no longer a non-stop, year-round job—farmers have a lot more free time.

— In many rural areas, income from working the land remains meager. Farmers do not want to settle for earning only enough for food and clothing after a year of hard work. Many opportunities for making money are drawing them away.

— The flourishing metropolises are attracting many farmers, especially the younger generation. They are increasingly discontent with monotonous rural life.

But the reason why farmers leave the land actually is very simple: China's land can no longer satisfy the requirements and dreams of 800 million rural people.

When the building of a new countryside begins, we cannot ignore those rural people who have left their land.

Training of Farmer Workers

At present, there are nearly 500 million rural laborers in China, and only 200 million agricultural laborers are needed to work the land. That means there are still nearly 300 million surplus rural laborers needing to find a way to make a living. Moreover, this surplus grown by more than eight million people every year. Where should such an enormous number of surplus rural laborers go?

◆ Ningbo government holding a job recommending and introducing meeting for rural youths.

The migration process started in the 1980s, when, for a while, many farmers worked in local township enterprises. Most of the farmers would leave their fields but not their hometowns and they looked for jobs and ways to make money nearby. With the quickening of the reforms and opening-up policy launched in 1978 many farmers traveled further away to provincial cities, the capital or the developing coastal cities. These big cities were in the process of development and construction, and so could provide farmers with more opportunities.

These farmers who have left their land are called "migrant workers." According to the "Investigation into Chinese Migrant Workers" published by the Research Office of the State Council in 2006, there are around 120 million migrant workers nationwide. If the rural laborers employed by local township enterprises are included, the total number of migrant workers stands at around 200 million people.

But to help these 200 million people quickly and painlessly find a job is a big problem.

The technical ability of these migrant workers determines their job security and their income. At present only 20% of rural laborers have received short-term vocational training, 3.4% have received elementary vocational and technical training or education, 0.13% have received intermediate vocational and technical education, while 76.4% haven't received any technical training at all. According to the Ministry of Construction, 32 million migrant workers work in the construction industry, with only 10% having received formal training. Over 70% of rural laborers in the United States, Canada and other developed countries have received vocational training.

In July 2005, government departments in Sichuan Province arranged for 600 local girls to go to Beijing to seek jobs as housekeepers. Once they had started work in Beijing residents' homes, they found it hard to adapt to the life and work in Beijing because of their cultural and technical disadvantages. There were many differences between them and their employers, such as the original places they come from, their economic background, their habits and their ideas. Only a week after their arrival, dozens of them left Beijing; after a month, as many as a hundred of them disappeared.

If this is the case with housekeeping work, which requires a relatively low level of culture, technical expertise and knowledge, it becomes obvious how difficult it is to transfer the rural labor force. This is the reason that technical training for the rural labor force is attracting more and more attention.

Since 2004, the ministries of agriculture, finance, labor and social security, education, science and technology and construction jointly implemented the

◆ The new students of the first free vocational school in Beijing reciting poems on the school opening ceremony.

"Sunlight Project for the Training and Transfer of the Rural Labor Force," providing various kinds of training to surplus rural laborers. By the end of October 2006, the Sunlight Project had trained a total of 8.3 million rural laborers, overseen the transfer and employment of 7.2 million people, with a training and transfer success rate of 86.7%. By participating in vocational and technical training under the Sunlight Project, nearly half of all trainees reached an elementary or higher level of vocational and technical ability. Most of them have found stable employment for one year or more. According to one county which followed up those who had participated in the Sunlight Project, farmers who received transfer and employment training get an average monthly income of 833 yuan per person, 400 yuan more than those doing farm work at home, and about 200 yuan more than migrant workers who have not received any training from the Sunlight Project.

In the past three years, the central treasury has invested 1.25 billion yuan in the Sunlight Project. The standard subsidy awarded to farmers participating in the scheme rose from 100 yuan in 2004 to 171 yuan in 2006. Supplementary funding provided by provincial-level treasuries exceeded 1.5 billion yuan, giving local authorities the impetus to offer vocational and technical training to more than 10 million rural laborers.

Providing Migrant Workers with Living Security

We must pay attention to the 120 million migrant workers who left their hometowns to work in cities. Statistics show that migrant workers generally account for more than 60% of people traveling over Spring Festival. The farmers spend most of the year working in cities. It is only at Spring Festival that they are all able to go home and reunite with their families and celebrate the New Year with their parents, wives and children.

The floating rural population's desire to escape poverty makes them an extremely hardworking group. In today's cities, high-rise buildings spring up from the ground, streets are neat and clean and markets are stable and flourishing—this is the result of the sheer hard work of migrant workers. Migrant workers take jobs that many city dwellers are unwilling to do. They are quietly doing their bit to improve urban residents' lives and their working environment. The overwhelming majority of urban sanitation workers, housekeepers and catering staff are migrant workers. Without them, whole cities would slow to a halt. In Beijing and other big cities, there is a serious shortage of housekeepers when migrant workers return home at Spring Festival. It can really affect residents' daily lives and the overall running of the city. They are the biggest group to have been

◆ On February 9, 2007, 130 migrant workers on a chartered plane back to Chongqing for the Chinese Spring Festival.

The Road to a New Countryside

◆ Migrant workers studying in an evening school in Nanning City, Guangxi Zhuang Autonomous Region.

truly absorbed into city life and they are also an important force in the drive for urbanization.

Although migrant workers have become indispensable in running the cities, they have sometimes come into conflict with the social systems developed in these cities over a long period of time. Cities are unable to offer migrant workers and urban residents the same benefits in education, healthcare and other areas. This formidable labor army, to a great extent, is still languishing outside the systems of modern employment. The result is that migrant workers lack certain employment guarantees, for example: minimal wage, fair compensation for labor, disaster relief, labor protection, job-training, education for their children, housing, healthcare, basic pensions and industrial accident insurance.

In recent years, the wind has changed and all sorts of employment services and preferential policies have been directed towards migrant workers.

The "Spring Wind Scheme" initiated by the Ministry of Labor and Social Security called on the nation's labor and social security departments to make use of the post-Spring Festival period to provide employment service for the large number of people seeking jobs in cities, so that rural laborers "have a way to get jobs in cities, and are not deceived when seeking jobs or accepting employment, and their labor rights and interests will be guaranteed." Labor service centers are springing up all over the country. They provide information services for migrant workers seeking employment. Many places are devoting themselves to, and, in some cases, have even solved, problems relating to non-local medical insurance and children studying in non-local schools. In recent years, railway departments have run special trains for migrant workers, making it convenient for them to return home. Banks offer migrant workers special bank cards and with favorable charges when they take money from the bank to return home.

In early 2006, the State Council published its "Suggestions for Solving Problems Concerning Migrant Workers." The paper set forth seven major new policies, calling for a solution to problems related to low wages and debt, better employment services and job-training, and the continuing improvement of social security for migrant workers.

In June 2006, the Ministry of Labor and Social Security said that within three years China would provide basic industrial injury insurance for migrant workers working in mining, construction and other dangerous enterprises. In addition, legal institutions across the country provided legal-aid for a total of 125,290 migrant workers, 65% more than the previous year. In September that same year, the Education Institute of Peking University started its experimental "School for Everyone" project geared mainly towards migrant workers. This shows that higher education has opened its door to migrant workers.

The shift and flow of labor is a natural trend caused by the development of the market economy and is one of the targets of social progress. During this process, however, the country's institutions must adapt to the new trend. The Chinese government is now constantly adjusting and perfecting policies and institutions to make sure migrant workers enjoy an easy transition and are absorbed into city life.

◆ Luo Yuhang, son of migrant workers from Sichuan Province, studying in Fujian Province.

Agricultural Industrialization Retains Farmers

The "Investigation into Chinese Migrant Workers" carried out by the Research Office of the State Council states that, for a long time to come, the majority of migrant workers will continue to flow into economically developed coastal areas and large or medium-sized cities. At the same time, however, it should be noted that over 70% of China's population lives in counties and surrounding regions, and these regions are responsible for over 50% of the GNP. When it comes to the transfer of labor, we should not neglect local channels. For the foreseeable future it will be necessary to promote the development of township enterprises and county economies to encourage the transfer of labor to these areas. Ninety percent of the rural labor force in Zhejiang, Jiangsu, Shandong, Guangdong and other economically developed provinces is transferred to local or nearby enterprises. A huge number of people must be transferred to cities and towns, but not everyone can go to large and medium-sized cities, a considerable proportion of them need to live and work in county towns or in towns below county level.

If the transfer of labor is to take the form of farmers leaving the fields but not their hometown, it is necessary not only to rely on the impetus given by local township enterprises— agricultural industrialization will play an increasingly large role. With agriculture gradually forming on a regional pattern, and the adoption of specialized production, large-scale operation, and business-like management, it is possible for the rural labor force to be transferred in an orderly manner. A very good example of this can be found in Shandong's Weifang, the birthplace of China's agricultural industrialization.

In Weifang, 12 counties and county-level cities have

given birth to 17 agriculture-dominant industries including Shouguang vegetables, Zhucheng livestock and Qingzhou flowers as well as more than 2,400 leading enterprises of various sizes. At present, over 3 million rural laborers are engaged in intermittent or long-term work in local leading enterprises, offering jobs to the entire rural labor force in the locality.

According to statistics from the Ministry of Agriculture, in 2005 China had more than 70,000 large-scale farm product processing enterprises, worth an output value of 4.2 trillion yuan and employing 17.85 million people. In terms of expansion and speed of development, the farm product processing industry is one of China's fastest growing "pillar industries." The Ministry of Agriculture has set several goals for the future development of China's agricultural product processing industry. It hopes to attain an average annual growth of 12% in development speed, reaching a ratio between the total output value of the processing industry and gross agricultural output value of over 1.5:1 by 2010. It also hopes to attain a transformation rate of 60% in farm product processing and an intensive processing rate of over 40% for the main agricultural products. It will offer special help to China's leading processing enterprises. These enterprises will be divided into two groups: those whose annual sales income exceeds 10 billion yuan and those whose annual sales income exceeds 5 billon yuan.

At present, Chinese township enterprises employ 140 million rural laborers, accounting for nearly 30% of the rural labor force. These rural laborers earn an average of over 1,200 yuan a year from township enterprises, one third of that earned by rural laborers overall. In addition, 50 million people are employed by private enterprises or are self-employed. The new plan for agricultural industrialization means that there will be even more farmers who are able to escape poverty and become wealthy without moving far from their homes.

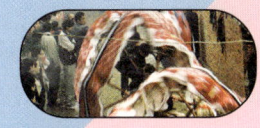

6

Who Cultivates Culture?

A village in Guangdong Province has four very impressive *quyi* (ballad singing) troupes who perform Guangdong opera. The lovers of Guangdong Opera enjoy the performance of these troupes while exchanging their own experience. The founding and development of these ballad singing troupes has brought new vigor to the villagers' spiritual and cultural lives. It is only a shame that relatively few people have joined these troupes and that mahjong is the main entertainment in the village. Most of the members of the four singing troupes are over sixty. When these people quit the stage, there will probably be no one to carry on the troupe.

On the one hand, very few young people take part in healthy recreational activities; on the other hand, traditional *quyi* troupes are going out of fashion. This situation is representative of the cultural predicament of many Chinese villages.

Rural Cultural Construction

In the building of a new countryside, the Central Government has created a fund specially to develop rural culture. Local governments have also allocated funds to support rural public cultural projects. At the end of 2005, the CPC Central Committee and the State Council jointly issued a document on further strengthening rural cultural work, calling for the development of various kinds of cultural activities oriented toward rural areas

Who Cultivates Culture?

◆ A young lady introducing ceremonial knowledge to people in Houyuzi Village, Shandong Province.

and farmers. With the government providing support through policy and subsidies, local people will organize cultural centers, reading rooms, film projection teams and theatrical troupes. This will make farmers largely responsible for rural cultural development and they will be given the same treatment as state-owned cultural

◆ Young women in Nanke Village in Shannxi Province showing the hand-weaved clothes, local folk handicrafts.

enterprises in such areas as land use, credit and industrial policy.

By 2010, in the construction of rural cultural facilities alone, financial support from the state and local governments will have made cinemas, cultural centers, libraries and other facilities a universal feature of rural China.

Through financial aid and rewards for county-level theatrical troupes which have served grassroots units over the years, the Ministry of Culture will encourage more county-level theatrical troupes to devote themselves to better serving people at the grassroots level. Soon it will not be necessary to take culture to the countryside: culture will be rooted in the countryside. The activities, organized by government departments, to take culture to the countryside are spreading like wild fire. In recent years, Henan Province has expanded its film projection scheme throughout the province. The province boasts 6,556 rural film projection teams who show 320,000 films every year. It has become important in enlivening rural cultural life. In 2005, the Cultural Department of Henan Province obtained a 2.4 million yuan grant from the provincial treasury with which it purchased mobile film projection vehicles, mobile film projection caravans, film projectors and film reels. It then distributed the equipment to 20 key provincial-level counties which were making effort to relieve poverty. Recently, Henan was named the nation's main experimental province in the reform and development of rural film industry by the State Bureau of Radio, Film and Television.

Apart from the government's efforts, there are other groups doing their bit to spread culture among China's rural areas. There are around 3,000 folk troupes in China's rural areas. Many troupes give hundreds of performances every year. Whenever there are weddings or funerals, temple fairs, major festivals and activities in rural areas, there will be a folk troupe performing before crowds of people and a hubbub of voices.

In rural areas of Zhejiang Province, you often hear

a gong marking the start of a performance. Many outstanding performers have become stars to the farmers of Zhejiang Province. Now Zhejiang has more than 400 folk troupes. They go deep into rural areas to perform *Yueju* opera, *Wuju* opera, *Huangmei* opera and other traditional operas. These operas either evoke traditional Chinese morality, or else tell stories closely related to farmers' lives, delighting and fascinating spectators. These Zhejiang folk troupes give 140,000 performances every year for farmers, and are very important in building a new rural culture.

These folk troupes often encounter different difficulties from government cultural departments, such as a shortage of finances or personnel. But on account of their profound affection for rural culture and farmers, they have survived and have become an important tool in developing rural culture.

Culture Promotes Economic Development

Promoting rural culture does not just nourish the minds of farmers; many places have local culture to thank for their simple and harmonious atmosphere and have reaped economic gains as a result.

In 2001, a girl named Zheng Bing from a village in Shanxi Province envied the rich and colorful cultural life of the city, so she organized an aerobics and dance class for female villagers in slacken seasons. At first it was met with opposition and sneers by many of the conservative villagers, but, due to Zheng Bing and some other women's persistence, more and more villagers began to support the group. Soon people started joining in with the activities. The villagers' cultural activities became increasingly varied. Zheng Bing began organizing debates, tugs-of-war, and chess games. A villager said that since the launch of these cultural activities, there was no longer any squabbling or ill-treatment of parents-in-law in the village. In 2004, Zheng Bing and other villagers established a farmers' association, to carry out a wider range of non-cultural activities. This organization, which was established as a result of cultural activities, has great influence with villagers and helps bring them together. Zheng Bing called upon villagers to clean up the garbage dump that had accumulated over a dozen or more years and led villagers in reinforcing all village roads. Things that could not be accomplished in several terms by the villagers committee were dealt with by Zheng Bing and her association.

In this way, the launch of cultural and recreational activities has quietly and gradually changed the mental outlook of a village and given impetus to the development of cultural and recreational activities in neighboring villages. Now, the farmers' association has a membership of more than 3,800 people over 35 villages of two towns. The association has set up five science and technology centers, one paint processing factory, one women's handicrafts workshop and one steamed bun kitchen. There is also a senior citizens association, a youth center and a healthy home council.

Farmers used to always complain about Gaobeidian Village on the outskirts of Beijing as it was covered with garbage. In 2002, because the land was needed for the construction of a key state project, over 153 hectares of cultivated land was requisitioned. Consequently, 810 farmers lost their land. Who would help save a village that was in such a state? That was when Gaobeidian people remembered the thousand-year-old culture of their village. Villagers turned their attention to the village's classical furniture and organized a street to sell distinguished classical furniture. Taking advantage of the culture of the thousand-year-old village, they quickly established themselves in the classical furniture industry. In the short space of several years, the number of firms dealing in classical furniture in the village increased 14-fold, and annual income from sales rose from the original few million yuan to 180 million yuan. The village became the center of the production and trade of classical furniture in Beijing, invigorating the village's economic development. In 2005, the village's total income was 1.25 billion yuan, with villagers earning an average of 16,000 yuan a year.

Later, in order to increase its attractiveness as a cultural destination and to lay a foundation for long-term development, Gaobeidian Village restored its time-honored Caoyun ("waterway transportation") temple fair, and organized a stilts team, a pushcart fair, a Yangko team, a choir, a drum team and other recreational and sporting organizations. Especially important was the revival of the art of Gaobeidian stilts performance. This type of performance has a 120-year history in the village but had completely died out. Not only did they perform in front of a Chinese audience, but also took their art to London and Sydney where they received a

◆ Villagers in Zhenhuli Village, the birthplace of Gan Opera, in Jiangxi Province, watching the opera in the rain.

◆ Miao People in Zhouxi Town in Guizhou Province celebrating the Lusheng Festival in the first lunar month of each year.

warm welcome.

Under governmental guidance and support, many villages close to scenic spots and historical sites have started marketing themselves as rustic attractions. They use local culture to attract urban residents to experience life in farming households. They can eat in farmers' homes, sleep on *kang* beds, see local opera and pick fruits in orchards. This has increased rural incomes and promoted cultural exchange between urban and rural areas. Some places have even turned rustic culture into a brand.

7

Seeking Dynamics from Farmers

◆ A villagers' representative voting on a local rule at the polling station in Nanjian Village, Zhejiang Province.

In the construction of a new countryside, state investment planning and participation is all important, but by the far the most important factor is farmers themselves. What do the majority of farmers think about the upsurge in rural development? What are they willing to do for the construction of a new countryside? And can they go about doing it?

A New Way of Thinking

When some villages in Liulihe Town in Beijing's Fangshan District replanted forests, farmers decided that, as that forest produces slow results, they would try to plant some more crops under the trees. It was a good idea but many farmers do not know what crops to plant. Some farmers planted grapes under poplars. Because the growth pattern of grapes is similar to that of poplars, it is impossible for grapes to get sufficient sun, and so it is not very efficient. When a professor from the China Agriculture University came to the village to provide technical support, he suggested that villagers change to planting garlic. Garlic grows from the end of October to early May, which is precisely when poplars lose their leaves, so the two do not interfere with each other. After the professor's suggestion was put into practice, villagers saw some fairly big economic benefits. One villager was very grateful: "Although I deal with the land everyday, I'm still not up with a lot of agricultural science and technology."

Farmers do not just need to make agriculture more scientific; in order to build a new countryside, they must first change their way of thinking.

Wang Jiwei, president of a farmers' cooperative in Huzhai Village, Lankao County, Henan Province, has personal experience in this area. In 2000, Wang Jiwei took the lead in forming the Huzhai Village Crop and

Livestock Association in an effort to grow sought after vegetables. Wang went out to investigate the market. The villagers, who were joining a cooperative for the first time, planted 1.5 hectares of Western pumpkins. They tasted the fruits of their labor four months later— it was a great success. In 2004, the cooperative expanded to 7 hectares. There had, however, been a complete turnaround in the market. Faced with rapidly declining prices, the cooperative farmers were at a loss for what to do and could not reach an agreement on how to deal with the produce. That year the association was dissolved. Zheng Bing, head of the farmers' association in Yongji City, Shanxi Province, had a similar experience. Soon after the Women's Handicraft Association was set up, products were put through quality testing. The tests showed 38 of the 200 staff were making sub-standard products. As they did not understand market regulations, when Zheng Bing asked them to remake the products, the farmers insisted that Zheng Bing was just trying to humiliate them. Zheng Bing now says that farmers have to change their way of thinking. Only then, will they be able to adapt to the market and move towards development.

The No. 1 report of 2006 of the Central Government states that in order to build a new socialist countryside it is urgent that we "train new-style farmers who are educated, understand technology and are business

◆ Farmers in Nantong City in Jiangsu Province competing in the First Farmer's Internet Knowledge Contest.

oriented." The two stories mentioned above illustrate that only by training thousands upon thousands of highly qualified new-style farmers is it possible to transform the large rural population from a disadvantage into an advantage—from a burden into a valuable pool of human resources. In this way the new countryside will offer twice the results with only half the effort.

In 2006, the Ministry of Agriculture named the "Plan for a Million Technical Secondary School Students" as one of its 15 measures to be implemented to help farmers. This plan, by relying on agricultural technical secondary schools, agricultural multimedia schools, and other institutions, will train one million people for work in the countryside over a period of 10 years. They will be trained in crop cultivation, livestock breeding, processing, business management, craftwork, agricultural science and other skills.

Village Autonomy and Democratic Management

When people go to Panjiabin Village in Xiuzhou Prefecture of Zhejiang Province they will find straight,

smooth cement roads running right to the door of every household. These houses are all attractive and practical. A stream meanders round green trees which thicken into a forest: the eye is met with a scroll of rich and beautiful landscapes.

"Whatever the village wants to do, it will hold a meeting to solicit our views. The village usually acts on our suggestions. When we work together, is there anything we can't accomplish?" raved Ye Ahming, a resident of the village. Zhou Zhichuan, old Party member, chimed in: "Of the principles laid out for the building of a new countryside, our village definitely meets the one about 'democratic management.'"

▲ The villagers' waist-drum band performing at the Jiangyan Cauliflower Festival in Jiangsu Province.

As early as in 1998, Xiuzhou Prefecture started making village affairs public and introduced democratic management. At first this system was implemented in a few experimental areas, affected relatively few people, and had to be enforced. Now it has become universal, and people happily abide by its rules. Its operation continues to be systematized and standardized. Over 90% of villages have been made model villages for their achievements in autonomous management. In 2002, Xiuzhou Prefecture was named "Model Prefecture for

◆ Ying Xiaoping, an agriculture technician in Ningbo City in Zhejiang Province, introducing vegetable growers how to prevent diseases and pests.

Village Autonomy in Zhejiang Province" by the Civil Affairs Department of the province.

Panjiabin Village's move towards autonomy is a good example of the development of village autonomy in China. There are only five people in Panjiabin Village Committee, but they are able to handle all the village's affairs. Civil affairs, accounting and statistics are all handled by the village head; village finances and social insurance are handled by the chairperson of the women's organization—everyone has several responsibilities. The village's current managing body was elected in a secret ballot by 1,400 voters.

It is the villagers themselves who elect the managing body and who manage village affairs. Every expense of over 1,000 yuan must be discussed by all members of the village managing body, and the manager, certifier and examiner cannot be bypassed. Major activities involving village and financial affairs must always go through three-level democratic consultation. First, the village managing body will hold a discussion, putting forward their initial ideas and drawing up a plan; this will then be discussed at a meeting of party members and team leaders and further ideas will be solicited; finally the plan will be put to vote at the village representatives' conference. For construction projects such as road building, after the plans have been ratified, the village will publicly invite tenders.

In order to make village affairs more transparent and democratic, Panjiabin Village has made a "Four Votes and Two Announcements" account book. Six such thick account books are provided for villagers to consult. If they look at the entry for a resolution approved at a village representatives' conference, villagers can see that the conference had discussed such sensitive financial affairs as the final account of 2004 and the collection of the village's public welfare funds. An attached sheet bears the signatures of 35 villagers.

The first villagers' committee was founded in 1980. By the mid-1980s, most places had set up villagers' committee organizations. At present, such grassroots democratic institutions are the most widespread institutions of their type in rural China. They are playing an important role in the building of a new countryside.

Promoting Autonomy

Immediately after the founding of New China in 1949, the countryside was very poor. Peasants frequently did not even have enough food and clothing, and the state did not have much money to support rural construction. But due to their insurmountable courage peasants were able to change the face of their towns bit by bit. The foundations for the ditches, water dikes, small reservoirs and roads we have now were laid at that time.

Today, although China already has the economic

◆ Farmers in Ganjing Town of Shannxi Province reading books of agriculture science and technology.

base to help develop the countryside, it is impossible for the government to do everything by itself. Although the construction of a new countryside is a national strategy, if it is to be fully implemented, it is still necessary for the farmers to show their previous energy and spirit in building a new home for themselves.

Dongwa Village in Pinggu District, Beijing, invited experts to come and work out a plan for the construction of a new countryside. When drawing up the plan, experts went over every step with villagers. On the question of whether the village should have a cobblestone road or a cement road, villagers and experts were divided. Experts were inclined towards cobblestones, thinking that it would better protect the ecological environment, while the villagers preferred cement, as it is convenient for transport. The elderly and the disabled, especially wheelchair users and their family members who look after them, favored building a cobblestone road. Some villagers also recognized that a cobblestone road would be convenient for wheelchairs— they would not slip on hills on rainy and snowy days. There were many other differences of this kind when making plans, but through consultations and meetings the verdicts they finally reached were fairly unanimous. A village cadre said that, in the future, Dongwa Village should adopt this method of management so farmers feel they are masters of their own affairs, stimulating villagers to build a new countryside.

In Tongxin Village, Yuexi County, Anhui Province, the heartland of Dabie Mountains, in winters gone by people either felled trees and burned them to warm themselves, went hunting, or drank wine round a hot pot to while away the time. But in the winter of 2006, the villagers took on different habits. Every morning, they would go to their fields and make preparations for next spring's plowing and sowing. Despite the bitter cold, people working the fields were a common sight. These changes were brought about by the villagers' mutual-aid fund for production and developments set up by the provincial treasury. The government gave money to those villagers who need help with production costs. The villagers reached an agreement on how exactly to spend this money. It was this "little bank," managed, directed and staffed by the villagers, which has provided many villagers with start-up funds needed for developing production. This system instilled the villagers of Tongxin Village with a tremendous energy.

There is an ancient Chinese saying: "Officials are responsible for making decisions for the people." However, in the building of a new countryside, the government does not want to "make decisions for the people." The planning process of Dongwa Village and the mutual-aid fund of Tongxin Village ignite farmers' enthusiasm for production and construction for the same reason: they both give farmers the right to be masters of

◆ Villagers in Yongshou County voting on a road-building project.

their own affairs. Farmers know their own homes better than anyone else and are most clear about what they need, so they are the most qualified to comment. At the same time as granting rights to farmers, these villages also handed responsibility over to them, driving farmers to participate in the construction of a new countryside.

Farmers' Views and Attitudes

At the end of November 2006, after conducting an intensive investigation of farmers' attitudes, requirements and suggestions concerning the building of a new countryside in Jiangsu, Hunan, Hebei and Gansu provinces, professors from the China Agriculture University completed their report entitled "Research on the Construction of a New Countryside from Farmers' Perspective." This report shows:

In order of most concerned to least concerned, the degree of concern shown by farmers in the five aspects of construction of a new countryside is as follows: development of production, a higher standard of living, democratic management, improvement to rural customs and habits, and improvement to the living environment.

— Development of production: agricultural production was the main topic of discussions with farmers. What farmers need most is financial support.

— Higher standard of living: farmers are most concerned about increased wages. The most urgent matter is for the government to solve the problem of school fees.

— Democratic management: although this item is placed third in terms of level of concern, it is the item that farmers are least familiar with. This shows that grassroots democracy must be further developed.

— Improving rural customs and habits: more than anything farmers would like is a village reading room; gambling is the practice they would most like to see cut out.

— Improving the living environment: the problem of roads and garbage is their great concern, while the work of making the villages brighter and modifying houses is not seen as urgent.

These are the general expectations of the farmers surveyed. Many of their ideas are probably not identical with those of the government and experts; and in some places there was great variation between those surveyed. How to fully win farmers over to the construction of a "new countryside" is a problem needing careful consideration and will be treated on a village to village basis. The government will offer active guidance, and farmers' wishes will be fully taken into account and respected. Only if farmers support the plan for a new countryside will they devote all their energy to its construction.

图书在版编目（CIP）数据

新农村建设从这里起步：英文/王太，赵经平，李海涛著；
梁发明译. －北京：外文出版社，2007
(和平发展的中国丛书)
ISBN 978-7-119-05133-8

I.新... II.①王... ②赵... ③李... ④梁... III.农村 - 社会主义建设 - 概况 - 中国 - 英文 IV. F320.3

中国版本图书馆 CIP 数据核字（2007）第 157300 号

作　　者	王　太　赵经平　李海涛
责任编辑	崔黎丽　薛　芊
英文翻译	梁发明
英文审定	John Mcmillan　徐明强
内文及封面设计	天下智慧文化传播公司
执行设计	姚　波
制　　作	北京维诺传媒文化有限公司
印刷监制	冯　浩

新农村建设从这里起步

*

© 外文出版社

外文出版社出版
(中国北京百万庄大街 24 号)
邮政编码 100037
北京外文印刷厂印刷
中国国际图书贸易总公司发行
(中国北京车公庄西路 35 号)
北京邮政信箱第 399 号　邮政编码 100044
2007 年(大 32 开)第 1 版
2007 年 1 月第 1 版　第 1 次印刷
(英)
ISBN 978-7-119-05133-8
17-E-3819P